Ivory Tablets
Of
The Crow

A Translation of the Dup Shimati

Warlock Asylum

ISBN-13: 978-1484812877
ISBN-10: 1484812875

:

Dedicated
to
The Teachings of the Path Itself

TABLE OF CONTENTS

The Birth of the Crow

Beyond the stars, beyond the darkness of the night they dwell. Into the realm of light they reside in stillness. Without need of the elements, for what is it? It is consciousness. The mere reflection of these words caused that which is self-aware to stare at itself in darkness. Yet, it remains whole. These are the Footprints of the Crow.

The witnesses of these thoughts are few. The mind must learn how to raise itself up and meet its reflection in the realm of light. The mere reflection of these words caused that which is no more to stare at itself in the light. Understanding these simple things is the basis of every creation, the Footprints of the Crow.

Why remain in emptiness? Take what is not useful and plant it in a good place. Waste nothing. I have learned many things in my years. A particular teaching was bestowed upon me by the gods and the progeny thereof. I became a wise one at a young age. It was difficult to obtain such knowledge, things forbidden were passed between the lines of fate until choice became my only resolve. This Path is Crooked. You read these words and think you understand, but still aren't aware of the secrets that must be kept by the cold of the fire.

Listen to my words carefully. Every battle is a creation. There is only one palace. It is the Dragon, but it is also called the Gate of Death in error by many who do not understand. You still do not understand. Look up at the heavens and see the darkness of the night that surrounds you. Is it not lifeless? While it may be spoken about in a manner that is common, it is still the home of the Wanderers and the Fiery Ones. Beyond this darkness is the place of eternal spirit in light. Very few have traveled this far. Some take faith in serving gods and demons. They receive a form of worship and think of a haughty existence. Their elements, though alive, are kept as idols that neither move or speak. Be not as these!

This is the Book of the Crow, Johuta, a daughter of ⴑ⋊

ⴑ⋊ ⴑ ⵟ ⵞ *, heaven. Herein lies the sacred text of the* ⵟ ⵜ ⵞ *containing the formulae of immortality and the lost arts useful only to the Children of* ⴑ⋊ ⵜ ♭ *.*
And surely the Magicians of the Secret Lands, not known to men, know the Footprints of the Crow, and those who observe them. Take special care not to change these instructions that I give unto thee by one letter, for in its perfection is its initiation.

Before the creation of man there existed a world beyond worlds, whose inhabitants built a great dwelling place in the Seas far beyond time. These cities were indeed a sight to behold, and special care was taken to ensure that each brick was nothing less than a fiery crystal, or a precious metal, engraved with mysterious symbols that could not be touched. Every day the fiery ones labored and toiled using only their eyes and thoughts as tools. Every night the Goddesses nurtured the scorpionic-architecture of these monuments and temples in their dreams. The Waters were One. Every pleasure in life was found in life itself, and the fiery ones saw that everything was good.

The fiery ones found much joy in the powers of arousal and spoke amongst themselves about creating a Space between the Spaces. They summoned a great scientist, who is skilled in a form of alchemy that is strange. His name is that of the

Quf.

Quf agreed with what the fiery ones had spoken concerning the creation of a world that exits in time. He went down to the River of Shadows and dipped his finger in the Egu. With one drop of water he created a stone that rested between the worlds of death and immortality.

The fiery ones built great cities inside the stars that shine in the Land of Shadows. But Yuvho saw the brightness of the Earth and took up residence in its Sun. Later, he constructed Seven Gardens on Earth, each resembling a city that exits inside the world that stands outside of time. The Army of Yuvho descended upon the Earth in Seven Dreams, Shamuzi being the first among them.

Finally after settling the Earth, they observed the cycles, which occurred in the Land of Shadows. The fiery ones calculated the times that the veils opened and closed, during the creative and destructive cycles of the Earth. The Fahmu could see the history of man before he was created and the end of all flesh.

So it was that man was created in the Earth and the Gods and Goddesses dwelt alongside man in the City of Vasuh, even begetting young upon mankind. And the Gods took their offspring, who were begotten by them, from amongst the daughters and sons of men. They taught them the customs and traditions of the fiery ones, and some of these, it is said, were even called Yuvhoa.

The fiery ones, after seeing the motion of the Earth and the recurrent destruction of man's civilizations, made an elixir to preserve their offspring and the faithful priests and priestesses who honored the sacred rites. The elixir is found in jade and somehow connected to the fruit of a woman during certain times of the moon.

The fiery ones created a beast named Muh, who is known as the Heavenly Bull in the legends of men, and they filled his veins with the jade elixir. The beast came to life and was able to send foretelling dreams and miraculous powers to the offspring of the fiery ones. The beast was placed in a region that is not visible to the eyes of men for fear that some of these would try to gain power over it. It is said that the name of this place is called Vasuh and Ut, the twin cities of water and fire, recorded in the histories of men, as a life tree. The children of the fiery ones are called Hahun, They hear the voice of their forefathers resonating throughout the societies of men. ↳ ! But during the beginning of the last age, certain priests, who were mortal, felt resentment against the children of the fiery ones. They learned the blasphemy of damnation and would recite the incantations and spells in reverse, which closed the doors to the outer worlds, while deceiving the children of men by their showy display and righteous character. Their deception and trickery is not easy to say in words, but it can be known because of their belief in one god.

Before the Throne of Quf lies an eternal flame called the Oracle of Fire. The Oracle says that when Muh rises men will be filled with pity and ready to rage war against the gods, but man will not prevail, neither will the priests of men who have betrayed our sacred ways, the sons of Aho.

After the last destruction, Yuvho created a fine image of man to inhabit during his visit to Earth. He gave instructions to the Yuvhoa and the Zhee to ensure the restoration of man's civilizations and withdrew the Difu from the world that exists in time. It was during this time that his passion was aroused by the Goddess Viyah. Yuvho employed a mortal king to build a temple for Viyah and himself, called Ioxna. Afterwards, he administered tasks to the Zhee, concerning Muh.

Yuvho remained on Earth for a little while, and he knew his wife Viyah, who bore him a son named Shara. And Shara took Shamhat as his wife, who bore him a daughter named Dakha. And Dakha married the mortal named Sheba from the land of Mu. And Sheba knew Dakha, and Dakha bore him a son named Mezek. And Mezek grew in wisdom and conquered many lands. He was a renowned one among the generations of men and found favor in the eyes of the gods. He taught the rites of the sacred fruit found in the pleasure of women. He is known to some as Malukedek.

And Ryhu bore Mezek a son named Shupu. After Ryhu gave birth to Shupu, Mezek lived for seven-hundred years more and was taken by the Fiery Ones to live in the World that exists outside of time and space. It was during this

time that the Veils of the Heavens were no longer seen by
men, and the Zhee only spoke with their children, who still
lived in the societies of man, which was done with great
care. And Shupu became father to Muku after three-
hundred years. And Muku became father to Xuz. And Xuz
was skilled in the ways of war. He traveled across the
waters of many lands and acquired a great deal of
knowledge concerning the forgotten things. Some say that

he was an immortal and would worship him as the ﾚ ﾚﾟ
ﾚﾟ ﾚﾟ .

One day Xuz decided to take a journey to the land of the
Orientals. During his travels Xuz fell sick, due to the
extreme cold, a task that is difficult for some men traveling
from Zuho. Xuz took refuge in a cave, hoping that the cold
wind would cease and fell asleep with only a portion of
food for day left, being that his company abandoned him.
He awoke in fear from the sound of coming footsteps.
Shortly after, a woman appeared with a fresh pot of stew
in her hands and a drawn sword. She was a beautiful
maiden with long black hair and full lips, like the flowers
that last for one season. The woman spoke to Xuz in a
language that he could not understand. She sat down next
to Xuz and fed him the stew with one hand while holding
the sword by his throat with the other. But when Xuz
revealed himself to her, the woman was astonished to see a
man with black armor. She trembled with fear, thinking
that he might be an emissary from the other worlds. She
withdrew her sword and stayed with him for some time.
She taught him the mysterious language of the Orientals
and their knowledge of certain plants and how to heal the
body. Eventually, Xuz took the woman, whose name is

ᚻᚱᚻᚱᚻ ᚦ ᚹᚻ - ᚻᚱ ᛚᛟ ᛚᛟ , moo-ah-moo-ah-eek-hss-you-mmh-ha-eh-ph-moo-ah-eehzz-eehzz, Lady of Heaven, the Warrior-Priestess, as his wife. She is the one

that the kings of the East would later call the ᚻ ᚹᚻ ᚹᚻ

ᚦ and would boast about being a child of her. But know that these things had not occurred at the time of her meeting Xuz. Xuz came to know Nudzuchi , and she bore him a daughter, Johuta, also known as the Queen of Stars.

After the birth of Johuta, the people in the village began to make gossip, concerning Nudzuchi, and accused her of practicing necromancy, since Johuta, like Xuz, wore black armor. The people began treating Nudzuchi like an evil spirit. So Xuz took his family up to the mountains for a short while, teaching Johuta the wisdom of the lands that he acquired during his journeys and their mysterious languages, also the path that connects many lands, which were unknown to merchants during that time.

Xuz decided to take a journey with the men of the boats and eat the fish of certain waters. While traveling through the mountains, he met a fisherman who gave him some fish in exchange for the fruits he took with him for the journey. Xuz was happy as he expected that he would return home a day earlier.

While walking through the mountains, he heard a great wind, but there was no breeze. He decided to climb a tree and wait. Some hours past, and he decided to climb down from the tree, when he saw Johuta and Nudzuchi practicing the mysterious arts. On seeing these things Xuz revealed *some of the customs and secrets of the fiery ones to his wife and daughter. Xuz and Nudzuchi taught Johuta all the things concerning the forgotten knowledge of the fiery ones, which she kept faithfully.*

The Nine Books of Dreams

I have copied these words faithfully as my Father instructed. They must be remembered for all that which is remembered is alive. If a thing is not remembered it cannot be put into operation. Long before my Father and I returned to the land, we learned of fools who read, but do not remember. They were deceived by spirits of the grave and promised many things which never came to pass. The knowledge you possess is the knowledge you remember. If it has not been remembered then it is borrowed, and will be taken away and searched for again and again.

The following are the Footprints of the Crow, who some men call the Dehfu, Books of Dreams. It is only by proper use of this language can one access the realms of knowing. Take these words with caution. Only exercise them after they are remembered:

(1st) Zhee. It is the first letter appearing in the Vasuh language. It means light of the goddess. Pronounced eehzz.

(2nd) Aum. It is the second letter in the language of Vasuh. It can be used to carry the powers of the first *symbol to any distant location. It can also be used to send and read the thoughts of others. Pronounced moo-ah.*

(3rd) Tuu. It is a symbol of protection and increases vitality. It is the third letter in the holy language. Nothing more can be said about this symbol. Pronounced oot

(4th) Hmu. Increases sexual energy and the eyesight. It is the fourth letter in the Vasuh language. Some have used this letter to travel to other worlds. Pronounced you-mmh-ha.

(5th) Bnhu. It is the fifth letter in the Vasuh language, and controls all things concerning the increase of one's wealth. It can also connect the user to the language of plants, and knows how to heal the internal organs of the body. Pronounced whoo-nn-bee.

(6th) Phe. It is the sixth letter in the language of Vasuh. It affects the quality of the emotions and useful for the arts of levitation. Pronounced eh-ph.

(7th) Nzu. It is the seventh letter in the language of Vasuh. Can be used as a protective shield, or to heal cuts and wounds. Pronounced ooh-zz-nn.

(8th) Iewhu. It is the eighth letter in the language of Vasuh. It is used in initiating one to the divine energies of the stars. Pronounced ooh-wel.

�५ (9th) Shki. It is the ninth letter in the language of
the Vasuh, and pertains to putting someone in a jar, or a
gate, or a vessel. It can also be used to send death energy
into an event, person, or object. Pronounced eek-hss.

This formulae was given to me when I first made my oath
to The Fountain of All that Dwells Beyond This World. It
is simple, but must be said one day after another for nine
days. It is called the ooh-zz-nn-eehzz-ooh-zz-nn, eek-hss-

eehzz-eh-ph, �५ ᐸᐅ�५ �५ ᐸᐅ〴 , the Soul of Fire,
known to the ancient by the names of many goddesses, and
it takes up residence in the flesh.

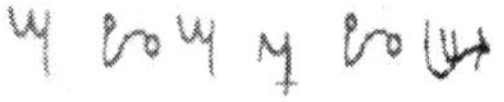

And this formulae must be memorized before its practice.
One day after the next it must be called for nine days. The
mantra must be recited when the invisible fire moves
through the body upon the breath. Remember, it is a mental
fire and the mantras are the letters and the letters are the
books and each book is a dream, both above and below.

"Eehzz-moo-ah-oot-you-mmh-ha-whoo-nn-bee-eh-ph-ooh-
zz-nn-uh-wel-eek-hss"

And these words must be recited in the position of the
formulae given and according to each wheel they represent
in the body. It is when the fire of the mind is imagined over

they head that the ᐸᐅ is seated at the crown of thy head.
And the fire of the mind will descend down to each
chamber, even the two of the world under. Know that

when the fire of the mind reaches the �५ , where all things

pass from the body, then it must rise back to the crown upon thy head.

This is the law of the time.

The Call of the Guardian Shamuzi

Few have been led down the Path of the Nine Dreams, for virtue is imperative in these worlds. The spirits show not their true faces to men, so they weep in horror. But for those who are pure in heart, there is beauty in these worlds. But the Path is difficult to find, and it is therefore necessary to call Shamuzi to guide you through the Dream of travel.

And the Shamuzi will protect thee from harm and the unknowing voices that will try to enter the mind. And do not be alarmed by her appearance when she comes to greet thee and stand by thy side. Now the lower part of the Shamuzi is like a horse and the upper part is that of a beautiful woman with long golden hair. Its eyes are like those of a cat and in its teeth are the fangs of a bat. However, its spirit is pure as a small child, for innocence is a valuable treasure that has long since been forgotten.

The Shamuzi, once called, will teach thee many strange and wondrous things. And the prayer, The Soul of Fire, must be sung with salt water sprinkled around thee. The place must be clean. And once the Soul of Fire operation has been performed, thou must call Shamuzi and ask her to lead thee to The Fountain of Life. Such is her call:

moo-ah- you-mmh-ha- you-mmh-ha-Shamuzi ⤳ ⅌ ⅌
Come Shamuzi!

you-mmh-ha- you-mmh-ha-moo-ah- eek-hss Shamuzi ⅌
⅌ ⤳ ⅄ Come forth Shamuzi!

moo-ah- you-mmh-ha- you-mmh-ha; ⤳ ⅌ ⅌ Come!
eek-hss- eehzz-eh-ph; moo-ah-eehzz-moo-ah ⅄ ℭ ⒲
⤳ ℭ ⤳ Angel dwelling in the brightness! you-mmh-
ha- you-mmh-ha-moo-ah- eek-hss Shamuzi ⅌ ⅌ ⤳
⅄ Come forth Shamuzi! moo-ah-moo-ah-eh-ph-you-mmh-
ha ⤳ ⤳ ⒲ ⅌ Protect Shamuzi! moo-ah-eehzz-
eehzz; eehzz-moo-ah-oot- whoo-nn-bee-eehzz; moo-ah-moo-
ah- you mmh-ha- uh-wel; eh-ph-moo-ah-moo-ah-oot. ⤳

ℭ ℭ, ℭ ⤳ ⧺⋁ ♦ ℭ, ⤳ ⤳ ⅌ ℭℴℴ, ⒲
⤳ ⤳ ⧺⋁ Lady invoking Holy Dream, moo-ah- you-
mmh-ha- you-mmh-ha-Shamuzi ⤳ ⅌ ⅌ Come
Shamuzi! you-mmh-ha-eh-ph-eh-ph- ooh-zz-nn; moo-ah-
eehzz-oot- you-mmh-ha-moo-ah; moo-ah-eehzz-eek-hss-
moo-ah; moo-ah-oot-oot-eh-ph ⅌ ⒲ ⒲ ⅄ ; ⤳ ℭ
⧺⋁ ⅌ ⤳, ⤳ ℭ ⅄ ⤳, ⤳ ⧺⋁ ⧺⋁ ⒲ Bring forth
magic to crown! you-mmh-ha-eh-ph-eh-ph- ooh-zz-nn; moo-
ah-moo-ah- you mmh-ha- uh-wel; moo-ah-moo-ah-eehzz-oot
⅌ ⒲ ⒲ ⅄ , ⤳ ⤳ ⅌ ℭℴℴ; ⤳ ⤳ ℭ
⧺⋁ Bring forth Holy Energy! you-mmh-ha- you-mmh-ha-
moo-ah- eek-hss Shamuzi ⅌ ⅌ ⤳ ⅄ Come forth

Shamuzi! moo-ah-eehzz-you-mmh-ha-eh-ph-eek-hss-oot;

५२ ७० ⇇ ७↦ ५ ╫✓ *It is done!*

These operations must be sung in the light of the Goddess of the Sun. The Sun is a keeper of the records of men and sees all that occurs. And these words must be committed to the memory of thy heart, but can be recited before. And Shamuzi is the spirit that gives the Sun its power.

And it may be that Shamuzi may come upon thy singing of the song. But if she does not come the first time, keep singing until it is so one day after the next for three days.

The Sword of the Ninzuwu

Know that every civilization comes into this world in the
manner of the Unborn. Each city exists in a place not
known to time and then descends upon the realm of man as
a kingdom, through some act of war, or a great migration.
Do not worship these things like men do, for it is a
forbidden art which keeps the soul bound to useless things.

It was so that upon the journey of dreams one may
approach old civilizations, some in the earth and others
that have vanished. Know that their gods and spirits may
try to tempt thee in dreams, but thou must remain pure.
And this world is full of Wanderers, those without spirit,
for they know not true joy.

Seek then the Dream of the Ninzuwu. The Ninzuwu have
the stature of a man and that of a woman. It is a
mysterious race. Their height is over twelve feet tall and in
front they appear as a woman, and when they turn about,
thou will see a face and body of a man upon their backside.
They carry no emotion and walk with bright copper skin
and white wings that extend the length of a man's arm.

And when you receive the Dream of the Ninzuwu, you
must vow to return to their realm and take refuge and
service among them, even upon earth they will watch over
thee for life.

It is the Sword that they will give to thee in Dreams. Know that the realm of the Ninzuwu is a place of mirrors above and below, side by side. It is a world of reflection, but the Ninzuwu walk about in this Dream as upon solid ground.

There is much knowledge in this realm, for when the Sword in given to thee in the dream, one can read the thoughts of others and the moments of life become long. The planets and stars will speak to thee in dreams.

And the Ninzuwu are the Caretakers of Stars in this World. It is said they were given authority over such, even that of Shamuzi, who must accompany you on the journey.

When thou has made ready for the Dream, perform the Soul of Fire prayer and call Shamuzi in song, then recite the Hymn of Ninzuwu:

Priests and Priestesses of Ninzuwu come!
From the Dream of the Great Circle of Stars come!
Ninzuwu, Realm of the Foretelling Knowledge, open!
Ninzuwu, Realm of Divining the thoughts of Planets and Stars, open!
Dream of the Sacred Mirror come upon me!
Ninzuwu, Winged Ministers of the Stars, come!
Ninzuwu, Rulers of the Seven Planes of Being teach me your Ways!
Ninzuwu, Counselors of the Zodiac, come!
I call the Ninzuwu in Love and Honor!
Share with me the Sword of Knowing!
Share with me the Sword of One Who Can Divine the Thoughts of Others!
I ask for the Gift of the Sword in Purity of The Dream!

Moo-ah-eehzz-oot-you-mmh-ha-moo-ah; eehzz-you-mmh-ha-moo-ah-eek-hss; oot-eek-hss-oot-eehzz; eh-ph-eh-ph-eek-hss-moo-ah-oot; you-mmh-ha-whoo-nn-bee-oot-eh-ph.

Ninzuwu with the Dream of Anointing, come!

This is the Hymn of Ninzuwu and it must be said for nine days, one after the other. The Ninzuwu know well the Path of Dreams. During these days of Calling, the rays of the Sun will anoint thee. The Ninzuwu may visit the person of these operations in physical form, usually as one ripe in years. They also speak through beautiful birds and plants. This is all that can be said about the Ninzuwu. It is a mysterious knowledge connected with the gifts that must be obtained in the Dream.

Opening the Sea

The Opening of the Sea must precede all operations given with the formulae listed herein. It is the Art of Fire and Water, which began in the cities of Vasuh and Ut. It was practiced by the god Quf. It is a simple formulae, but most necessary:

५⋗५⋗५ ⟋ ७⋗ ५⋗५ ७⋗ ♂ , ५⋗५⋗
७⋗ ⟋

Heaven-water, Protect

५⋗५⋗५ ⟋ ७⋗ ५⋗५ ७⋗ ♂ , ५ ℮०५ ,
५⋗५⋗७⋗ ⟋

Heaven-water, fire, Protect

Spirit of Vasuh, bless thy abode!

Spirit of Ut, bless thy abode!

And these words must be recited when the salt water is placed on the ground in a circle. If thou doesn't have the elements, it is only necessary to recite the formulae and to use the water of the breath and to create a wind about thee. Remember the breath is composed of fire and water too!

Know that all things exist in water, and that water is the space that the Dream exists in. Fire is the power that radiates its influence over the Dream, and the ancients would create "gods" out of those that shine the brightest. However, these things should not by worshipped as such.

The Dream of the Fahmu

Know that when the Sword of the Ninzuwu is received, it must be used to cut the Grasses of the Fahmu. And the Fahmu have bodies like trees with skin of flowing waters. Their land is like a desert of the skies, but it is a bright place.

Now between the Dream of the Ninzuwu and the Fahmu is the desert of skies where the Brightness always shines. It is a field of crystals that stands about three feet in height. Each crystal that stands in your path must be cut down by the Sword. In your journey you will come upon a Fountain of Flames, which is guarded by two of the Fahmu.

Upon seeing the Sword of the Ninzuwu, the Fahmu will inquire about your passage and the way you came upon this dream. You must answer with the following mantra:

"Ooh-zz-nn-eehzz-ooh-zz-nn-moo-ah-ooh-zz-nn-ooh-zz-nn-moo-ah-ehzz-oot-eek-hss!"

It means "fire-life eat." These words must be recited three times a day for three days, and the operations of the Prayer of Fire and the Call of Shamuzi must be observed. The Fahmu will come to thee in a dream holding The Chalice of Fire. Take the Chalice and drink the Fire of Life for its nature is good.

It is written that an elder of mankind was offered to drink the Fire of Life, but was told by a spirit not to touch it. This advice cause the calamity for the whole race of man. Surely, this fool was chained by the wrath of magic!

The magic men practice is vain. Those who worship the gods of temples are deceived by spirits who falsely glance at them with a calming face. Their priesthoods go about collecting tax for some form of power that the people do not understand. There is no salvation in these things, but the haunting of ghosts.

Know that when thou have fixed the mind towards the mystical journey of dreams, you must heed the practices of purity. Otherwise, you will face the demons in dreams and have little power over the Gate of Life.

Once having drunk from the Cup of the Fahmu, and tasted the Immortal Fire, you must keep it on the person of your mind. It must be used and prepared to drink from the Fahmu themselves, for their skin is like flowing waters, and they often share the Fire Water with those that know the way.

And the Cup of Fahmu can be filled with the Immortal Fire anytime one pleases, but best to do so before one sleeps. Once filled, it can be used during the Day of an Endless Age. The formulae is not a difficult task, save to push the air, containing the fire, out of the body while one whispers

ᘳ
.

Know too, that the Fahmu often take the nature of trees

and can by spoken to through the mind, and when the ᒪᕈ
is vibrating upon thy lips.

*Know that the Power of the Fahmu is found in the arts of
healing. They will teach thee many things concerning such,
and the skilled use of the breath in this regard.*

*The Fahmu speak through things that exist in field, also in
the trees. They can be spoken to through the Lake of
Dreams. This is what is said of the Fahmu.*

Quekanuit

Quekanuit is the said to be the Empty Space of the Warrior. It is a place that is empty of images and things usually perceived by the mind.

When the spirit enters Quekanuit the mind of thee will take a thousand forms. It is because of this reason that many call it the Dream of the Same Faces.

Know that when you enter this realm, thou will see an army of souls, and each soul is a deed that thou has performed in life. Some of these souls will be sad and others are happy. Some deeds will lust after their own selves. Every deed that one has performed will be seen by one, whether it be good or bad.

It is for this reason that many turn back from themselves and fear the journey. But do not be of this sort. And the Army of Deeds will come together to form one tall man with no hair. In his face one can see the deeds that they performed in life flashing and moving about the skin of the face and over the body. It is then that the Word of Quekanuit must be said seven times:

"You-mmh-ha-eek-hss-moo-ah"

When the word is said seven times the Quekanuit will turn into a small child with blue eyes and very pale skin. His face will have a very calmly appearance and he will bring you into the land of young children. Do not enter this land for your journey must continue.

And the Quekanuit is an awesome test that must be entered from the Land of the Fahmu. There are many who come across the Quekanuit and know not the reason. These remain as children and awaken from the Dream of Quekanuit with the mind of a child.

Passing the realm of Quekanuit gives one better control over the energies of the heart and mind. And the Place of the Quekanuit must be entered from the Fahmu, else the mind will become like that of a young child for there is where the Sons of Confusion remain.

Once inside the Land of the Fahmu, after having drunk from the Fire of Life, thou mayest call upon the Quekanuit. The formulae to open this Dream, must follow the Song of Fire and the Calling of the Shamuzi, drinking from the Cup of Immortal Fire. Afterwards, it is best to say the name Quekanuit only twenty-one times. It is then that the realm of Quekanuit will fall upon the mind and heart.

Ayaqox

Ayaqox the Great Woman was known as a Seductress in the world before man. She often changes shape to appear attractive to the mind of an Initiate. Sometimes Ayaqox will appear as a handsome man to a woman full of desire. Other times, she will appear to the man of great vigor, as a beautiful woman with long black hair and the face of a praying mantis with green skin.

But the Ayaqox also has a tail for she is the Person of Lust, and few can understand her. She left this world and found her place in the Realm of Eternal Lust. Her dwelling place is full of clouds and flashes of lightening. It is said that even the ground She walks on will appear as the clouds of heaven.

The Ayaqox is able to discern the desires of others, their motives, even though they may be hidden. But, she is also the teacher of the price of lust and knows the karma that must be paid.

And the realm is strange. The voices of those engaged in all forms of sexual pleasures can be heard and seen as shadows all around thee. However, in order to obtain the Stone Bowl of the Eternity, one must remain pure for seven days while reciting the Lustful Words:

Ayaqox, Keeper of the Lustful Realm, Come!

Ayaqox, Woman Who Dwell in the Realm of Eternal Lust, Come!
Ayaqox, Hearer of Desire, Come!
Ayaqox, I have searched for a pure place in your land!
I have called forth your name with a pure heart and a pure spirit!
I seek your blessing by which thou grant thee with the Stone Bowl of Eternity!
Holder of the Keys of Pleasure!
Ayaqox, I have remembered your name!
Moo-ah-Aya-qoz-eehzz-moo-ah-moo-ah-ehzz-moo-ah-moo-ah-eh-ph-oot-moo-ah-oot-
You-mmh-ha-moo-ah-moo-ah-eh-ph-ehzz-eek-hss-moo-ah-ehzz-ehzz

The reciting of Lustful Words must occur for Seven Days upon which no desirous contact can be made. After the Seven Days have passed, Ayaqox will visit thee in a dream and give unto you The Stone Bowl of Eternity.

When you receive the Stone Bowl in the Dream, you must fashion one like it upon awakening. And the Stone Bowl has many secrets, but it must be written about elsewhere, save that it should be made large enough to hold the Fire that one must pray over. When the Dream has ended, Ayaqox will reveal the Door of the Pure Place to you.

Zasosu

Ayaqox will cast a Dream upon your mind. Pay close attention. In the vision, a large door will appear among the clouds, and it must be open. When you have seen these things know that one must prepare for the Zasosu.

The Zasosu can give one a desire or take it away. They are the Lords of Impatience and Hesitation, and rule men through such. Some men have stayed in the Realms of the Zasosu and never perform any new task. But the Zasosu can also increase the Will of a man and the strength they hold within their hearts.

And the Zasosu have the face of an old man with the body of a goat and black teeth. Their skin is covered with hair that is the color of snow. They walk on their hind legs and have wings of a bat. It is said that if you see a Zasosu flying in your dream, good luck is on the way.

It is a curious dream in which they live, for it is a land desolate of structure, a land filled with many mountains of fine crystal. It is a place that is full of temples that were never completed, and some these were destroyed due to lack of care.

When thou has entered the dream, you will look up at the heavens and the sky will be as night on one side and day on the other. When you have seen this sign in the heavens, you must build a temple and offer it as a station for the Zasosu.

You must bring the Land of Zasosu into your mind and build a Temple before them for seven days. And you will see the Zasosu laughing, for they speak through a strange laugh. But you must remain steady in thy work. Each day you will become stronger by the laughter of the Zasosu.

The Temple must be made from the precious elements that stand around thee in the Land of the Zasosu. Its foundation must be constructed from the rocks of fire that fill the land. Its walls should be set up with water and wind. Its roof must be made from the precious gems that you will find when digging in the sky. And for Seven Days you must repeat the Laughter of the Zasosu, which I have written down for thee:

"Uooh-wel-whoo-nn-bee-you-mmh-ha; eek-hss-oot-oh-zz-nn; you-mmh-ha-eek-hss-moo-ah; eh-ph-moo-ah-ooh-zz-nn; you-mmh-ha-oot-oot-eek-hss; moo-ah-eek-hss-eek-hss-moo-ah-oot; you-mmh-ha-moo-ah-eek-hss-you-mmh-ha; moo-ah-moo-ah-ehzz-oot; moo-ah-you-mmh-ha-you-mmh-ha"

And these words must be sung in laughter, for laughter is the only language that the Zasosu understand. These will bring comfort to thee in times of distress. It is said that the Laughter of the Zasosu is the Will of the Journey.

The Body of Iwuvh

After the completion of the Temple of Zasosu, one must find the Body of Iwuvh. The time of preparation will come upon thee in a Dream of Istu. After these things, one must perform the operation set for the journey.

Now it must be understood that the Realm of the Iwuvh is very unusual and difficult to perceive, for the things in this place, appear and disappear in the same place, consistently, and without fail. It is said that the foundation of all things in the Place of Iwuvh is lightening.

The Iwuvh, which reside in the Place of Lightening, and have bodies made of wind. The upper part is like that of a man or a woman with no hair. The lower part is like the Eyes of Men and it moves from one place to the next by turning its eye in that direction.

Now the Iwuvh are born from the intercourse between the storms of that land. Otherwise, they have no pleasure between themselves and are very peaceful.

The Iwuvh are born from the storms that occur in the land. When they perish, the Iwuvh return to the body of the storm and are born again. The length of their life is as long as a flash of lightening, but the Initiate must obtain the Body of Iwuvh and have intercourse with it, for the Eye that it sits upon is the Eye of Knowing.

The Eye of Knowing is the Lifting of the Veil. Once the Eye has been opened, strange yet beautiful things can be

seen in thy dreams and when thou awakens from this realm.
The Eye of Knowing must be obtained through intercourse
with the Iwuvh. And the Pleasure of these ones can only
be seen when the Iwuvh fall asleep in death. When this
time occurs the Eye of the Iwuvh will appear as the organs
of the hermaphrodite and must be experienced in that
moment, else its Body will be taken by the Storm and be
born again.

What can move as swiftly as the Serpent from the Sky? Is
a question that even the Ninzuwu have pondered in awe.
And the Opening of the Sea must occur. And the Prayer of
Fire must be performed. And the Call of the Shamuzi must
be made. It is then that you must take the fluids of your
own procreation and burn them in The Stone Bowl of
Eternity, singing as if in ecstasy:

Iwuvh! Iwuvh! Iwuvh!
I anoint the Eye of Knowing that is now inside me!
Moo-ah-ehzz- oot-you-mmh-ha-moo-ah; Moo-ah-ehzz-oot-
whoo-nn-bee-ehzz; whoo-nn-bee-oot-whoo-nn-bee-oot!
Dweller in Lightening. May I understand you Ways
May I make use of the Lightening Power Wisely!
Moo-ah-ehzz- oot-you-mmh-ha-moo-ah; moo-ah-eek-hss-
Iwuvh-moo-ah; ooh-wel-moo-ah-ehzz; oot-eh-ph-eh-ph-
you-mmh-ha!
Iwuvh! Iwuvh! Iwuvh!
I anoint the Eye of Knowing that is now inside me!
It is done!

After the Eye of Knowing has been called, it must be
recited three times a day for three days. Before this time,
when the fluids of procreation are being gathered and

released from the body, thou must recite the word "Iwuvh" nine times.

The Beast of Muh

The Sons of Aho have betrayed our ways
With their magical arts
But what more are magical books
Than the jurisdiction and procedures
Set down by kings.

Souls who come to know the different
Sides of themselves
Gave a name to each attribute
And these names became known
As gods among those who lack the knowledge

These kings live forever
Due to the ignorant worship
Of their natures
Thrown about thrones
These are the emotions of kings
That no longer remain in the body
But they dwell as emotions in all men

Know that the names of these gods
Are a formula
A binding between the king and his earthly subject
Worship not the feelings of kings

The Ivory Tablets of the Crow

Seek only initiation
For initiation is the only law that is just unto man

They appear as kind
They are worshipped in beauty
But their intent is evil
The Sons of Aho have betrayed our ways

In the beginning there was peace
And in the beginning peace will always dwell
So it was that the Ninzuwu rested in the beginning

It was during this rest
That the Sons of Aho deceived creation
The Sons of Aho performed the Art of Trickery
And required sacrifice from man.

The Sons of Aho are the emotions of the dead
After the spirit has left the body

Man was lost.
The Sons of Aho created a lie.
They posed as the creators of man
But the world is the creator
Made by the creator
Man is lost.

The Sons of Aho are the emotions of the dead
After the spirit has left the body

Thus, the journey begins with a circle
With a circle the journey never ends
This is the question of man
For he will never understand the answer.

Keep these operations described in practice always. Keep the condition of the heart focused on what is clean, for things outside of these take away the attention of many. Understand that when the Eye of Knowing has been opened, the Initiate will see the Eyes of the Beast in the Dream.

Now the Beast of Muh has the head of a squid with radiant skin, like the fire that glows in the woods. It walks endlessly around trees that appear to be made of snow, and the Land of Muh is filled with a blazing heat. Few have ventured into the Ages of Vasuh and Ut because of the Beast that resides therein.

It is a fruitless journey to think that one can defeat the Beast of Muh and live. The Initiate will only suffer a cruel fate if such operations were tempted. But do know that our Queen was able to do such by surrender.

Surrender is indeed a lost art, but is necessary before the Baptism of the Ancient One. Remember, the Powers of the Eye of Knowing are miraculous and good. Yet, in surrender are the understanding of the Operations and the Powers of the Path.

The Act of Surrender is a blessing for those who have endured the height of the path. When the Eyes of the Beast of Muh appear in the Dream prepare for the operation. And the Opening of the Sea must occur. And the Prayer of Fire must be performed. And the Call of the Shamuzi must be made. And these words must be recited seven times a day for three days:

"Moo-ah-moo-ah-ehzz-oot; moo-ah-ehzz-eh-ph-moo-ah-moo-ah; you-mmh-ha-you-mmh-ha-moo-ah-eek-hss; you-mmh-ha-moo-ah-moo-ah-eh-ph-ehzz-eek-hss"

Let the Initiate know that upon the release of the Words of Power that a Great Healing will occur. The Beast of Muh feeds off of the profanities of man. Nothing more can be said about the Beast of Muh.

It is so!

Johuta the Mirror

It is said that the true sons
Do not commit to worship
But a meal between thee and the spirit
Is the art of sacred things

There is much wisdom that can be gained
From a relative in this world
And in the Dream

Let the bond of Love
Be shared between these things
And do not worship that
Which you do not know
Without Love
There is no faith
Without Love
There is no profit in faith

Yet, the Baptism of the Ancient One must occur
For initiation is the key
There are others who possess
Keys of this nature
And these keys can be shared if they have
Entered the Dream in the same manner

Choose only those ones that
will engage in the work wisely
Initiation is the Key

Be cautious of those who
Invoke gods
They do not know
The Path is Simple

Stay with the Soul of Fire
It is a Prayer of Fire that has been preserved
From a time that was before time

It is the Power of Lightening
Crooked in its shape
It is the Prayer of Fire

The Prayer of Fire
Is the glance
When that which is Self-Aware
Stares at itself

Nine books in the Dream
Like a lightning bolt
It binds what is Self
To that which is Self

The Nine Books of Dreams
Contained the Water
When it was One
For nothing ever changes
In the Dreams of Chaos

Baptism of the Ancient One

The Dream will enter the mind of the Initiate as the waters upon the shore. It is a Dream of Water, for all are born out of Water, even Dreams. It is then that the petition of the Baptism of the Ancient One must be made to the Queen of Nyarzir.

Nyarzir is the beginning of the path, and it will teach thee the wisdom of the Nine Books of Dreams. Know that the Opening of the Sea must occur. And the Prayer of Fire must be performed. And the Call of the Shamuzi must be made, but also the Stone Bowl of Eternity must be used in this operation and all those that occur after Baptism.

Now the Nyarzir exist beyond the worlds of time, and never leave their abode. Therefore, a petition must be made to the Bride of Nyarzir.

And the Bride of Nyarzir has the body of a beautiful woman wearing a white dress without legs. The head is that of four faces. The face of the North appears a Woman of Age and is made of Lapis Lazuli. The Face of the East is that of a Virgin and is made of Diamonds. The Face of the South is that of a Child and is made of the finest Gold. The Face of the West is that of a Mother and is made of Onyx.

The Bride speaks with four voices of different ages and these are always in unison, as she flies as the birds of heaven with wings of an Owl.

The Ivory Tablets of the Crow

Now the Nyarzir is a world with Three Suns and a Green Sky. Every structure is made out of a precious jewel and the roads of the cities are as fine metals. And these cities all stand around the Shining Trapezohedron upon which the Bride of Nyarzir sits upon her Throne.

Nyarzir is a place of instruction for all sorts of miraculous things, and many workers of the mystical arts do often visit and pay tribute to the Bride of Nyarzir for she will teach thee many things in Dreams and the world where the body must breathe.

This petition must be read in the light of the Sun. And the Prayer of Fire must be performed. And the Call of the Shamuzi must be made, but also the Stone Bowl of Eternity must be used in this operation and all those that occur after Baptism.

Bride of the Four Faces of Nyarzir
Upon thee I lay bare all things
For thy Anointing!
Queen of Nyarzir, Water of Life, Rise up!
For thy Anointing!
Whoo-nn-bee-ehzz; moo-ah-moo-ah-ehzz-oot; moo-ha-ooh-zz-nn-eh-ph-whoo-nn-bee; whoo-nn-bee-ehzz; moo-ah-ehzz-moo-ah-ehzz-moo-ah; moo-ah-moo-ah-ehzz-ehzz-moo-ah; moo-ah-ehzz-moo-ah; you-mmh-ha-eh-ph-eh-ph-ooh-zz-nn; eh-ph-eh-ph-eek-hss-moo-ah-oot; moo-ah-ehzz-eek-hss-moo-ah;
Bride of Nyarzir, rise up!
Ehzz arise!
Moo-ah arise!
Oot arise!
You-mmh-ha arise!

Whoo-nn-bee arise!
Eh-ph arise!
Ooh-zz-nn arise!
Ooh-wel arise!
Eek-hss arise!

I am thee Ancient One!
Glory! Glory! Be unto Nyarzir!

After these things are said The Bride of Nyarzir will come
to thee in a Dream and fill thy body with the Nine Letters
of the Vasuh. And each Letter is a Book and each Book is a
Dream and each dream is a footprint of The Crow.

Wutzki

It is upon the Baptism of the Ancient One that yea will
take thy rank among the Ninzuwu. And the Nine Dreams
must be invoked by the fire in the Stone Bowl of Eternity.
And the Prayer of Fire must be performed. And the Call of
the Shamuzi must be made, but also the Stone Bowl of
Eternity must be used in this operation and all those that
occur after Baptism.

Do heed these words well. Many of the Ones before Time
can be called by the Stone Bowl of Eternity. It is good to
exchange a gift with all who come in spirit or in flesh. Some
say the Cup of Fahmu is most desirous. Others burn incense
of Frankincense and Myrrh.

Now the Cosmic Fire of Wutzki must be called in the Stone Bowl of Eternity. The space must be made pure by the Opening of the Sea and a careful study of the Nine Books of Dreams.

Wutzki, Lord of the Immortal Flame, Arise!
Wutzki, Illuminator of the Way, Arise!
Wutzki, make this place pure for Calling!
Wutzki, Mighty Power of the Ancients Arise!
Ooh-zz-nn-ehzz-ooh-zz-nn; moo-ah-ehzz-moo-ah-ehzz-
moo-ah; whoo-nn-bee-ehzz
Wutzki, Hand of Nyarzir, Arise!
Wutzki, treasure of the Mighty Fahmu, Arise!
Wutzki, it is Ninzuwu that summons thee!
Turn back the faces and voices of evil!
Ooh-zz-nn-ehzz-ooh-zz-nn; moo-ah-ehzz-moo-ah-ehzz-
moo-ah; whoo-nn-bee-ehzz
It is done!

Testimony of the Crow

The beginning of every journey is always in this time now. For many years I struggled between the sides of darkness and light. There is no freedom in these choices for they are not choices at all. Can an infant choose between its mother or father? There is no freedom in such things. Just take what is not useful and plant it in a good place. This is the only choice you have.

There is no sense of reasoning with these feelings. I have seen them possess the body of the unwary, causing fits of anger and all sorts of hypocrisies. And the power these feelings have over the body of man cannot be put into words. But when the spirit is torn from the body these feelings act on their own accord and will haunt another house of flesh.

Know then that these feelings keep the spirit a prisoner in the house of flesh. They will make a blasphemy of the mind, so that the spirit becomes a worshipper of the same feelings that bind him. They often change into the shapes of gods and make the mind its disciple.

There are also the feelings that inspire men. These too act as his gods. They seek to free the spirit from its slavery, but they are confused because the mind worships a false god.

Know that the Workers of the Miraculous Arts in the World Before saw these things in parable, and gave each feeling a name, thereby binding it to a particular function.

It was then that the spirit was free to rise up back to its throne again. Is it not written; "That what is Old shall replace what is New?"

What side must thou take between feelings if the spirit is still in bondage? There is no freedom in such things. Just take what is not useful and plant it in a good place.

It was then that the Workers of the Miraculous Arts would initiate the Children from Above into their ways. After the knowledge was acquired, the Children learned the art of giving a feeling a name, thereby binding it to a particular function. It was then that the spirit in the Children became the god over a hierarchy of feelings.

Now it came about that the Children began to write about these things in fables, even sharing some of the feelings that were bound, with other Children. These feelings acted as servitors for the Children, but were described in fables as gods.

Generations passed, and the knowledge of the Workers of the Miraculous Arts and the Children from Above became hidden. The meaning of these things was no longer understood. The people turned away from the formula, as it was said to be written by men who write fables. The Knowledge was lost.

It was then that man turned away from his true spirit. The feelings that once served man began to rise in power. Over time the spirit of man became enslaved to his feelings. Many lives were lost as the powers of the feelings over men began to grow. Man's history became filled with bloodshed and things loathsome to the flesh, causing a great noise.

The Ninzuwu heard the noise of pain and sorrow. They remembered the Oracle of Man and saw all the spirits that were held in bondage.

The Ninzuwu called their Children. The Ninzuwu sent dreams to awaken their Children. Now many of the Children saw the dream, but did not remember the formula. They wrote about such things in their Books of Fables. Among these Children the formula appeared as something connected with the dead.

The Ninzuwu sent dreams to awaken their Children once again. Some of the Children heard the call in a dream. Others remembered the formula, as something dead, but still saw it in dreams.

And the spirit is dead, but the mind dreams and worships that which is forbidden. Dreaming is for the spirit, not the mind.

It is during the Baptism of the Ancient One that the Goddess revives the spirit. It is like a child being born into this world. When the child is in the womb. It is in this world, but it is in the mother's body. When the child is born it must know how to take care of itself.

During your instruction and exercises, you are still in the womb of your mother. When you are born, you must learn how to exercise your own divinity. The one who knows everything is not divine. Remember, the true meaning of god is always connected to something unconscious. God is the spirit that acts on its own accord and there is where true freedom lies.

Tongue of the Ninzuwu

The following information pertains to the use of the mystical and sacred language of primordial forces that existed before the creation of mankind, also known as the tongue of the gods. An important aspect of the divine language that must be understood is that it is not limited to the reactionary process of sound. A sacred tongue is a telepathic process, as all experiences and impressions are. This is how everything in nature is able to relate to itself.

Originally, the gods taught their progeny a code of sounds with the intent to uplift man to the state of telepathic communication. The Genesis account of the Tower of Babel metaphorically reveals how certain Initiates used this form of communication in a corrupted way and because of this spiritual crime, a once unified esoteric school of science became fragmented. The linguistic code, used as a tool to raise the Initiate's way of thinking from man to deity was lost, and man's longevity was shortened by his use of fragmented forms of communication.

I must warn the reader that the use of the following by the uninitiated can be disastrous for it is an aid in employing the chthonic mind and one must first be initiated into The Cult of Nyarzir. The Vasuh script can be spoken in two different distinct styles, which we will expound upon further in our discussion. Below is a simple glossary of terms and that the Initiate would do well to understand as these words and objects as they appear to them in dreams. The list of term is as follows:

A

Abiding = shki-nzu
ability = hmu-tuu
about =aum-shki
above = lewhu-nzu-hmu
above the firmaments = lewhu-nzu-zhee
act, action = tuu-shki
add = shki-bnhu
admiration = phe-aum-tuu
age, adept, ages, = zhee-aum
all= zhee-shki-phe-tuu-tuu
all creatures = zhee-bnhu
always = shki-aum
am (I am) = aum-hmu-tuu
am (I am the lord your god) = aum-shki-zhee
amidst = nzu-phe
among = lewhu-nzu-bnhu
and= aum
angel = shki-zhee-phe
angle = phe-bnhu
another = lewhu-phe
appear = tuu-nzu
arise = bnhu-zhee
ark = shki-hmu-aum

B

balance = phe-lewhu
be, become = bnhu-tuu
beauty= tuu-nzu-shki-zhee
become = hmu-phe

begin = shki-tuu-aum
beginning = hmu-tuu-lewhu
in the beginning = phe-bnhu-phe
the beginning= croodzi, iaod
begotton = aum-nzu-zhee-hmu
behold = shki-nzu-phe
bind = shki-phe-shki
blood, blood of = phe-aum-nzu-nzu
breath, living breath = aum-hmu-zhee
bright = zhee-lewhu-aum
dwelling in the brightness= aum-zhee-aum
bring forth = hmu-phe-phe-nzu
brother = zhee-zhee-aum
the brothers = zhee-zhee-nzu-aum
building = lewhu-bnhu-hmu
built = nzu-tuu-phe-aum
burn, burning = zhee-shki-nzu-phe-bnhu
by = aum-tuu-aum

C

call, called = nzu-nzu-hmu
called, named= shki-bnhu-aum
cast = hmu-bnhu-zhee-shki
cast down = hmu-nzz-zhee-bnhu-shki
cattle = hmu-aum-nzu-shki-nzu
cave = shki-hmu-lewhu-nzu-zhee
center = zhee-bnhu-zhee
chamber = aum-phe-phe-aum-zhee
circle = lewhu-nzu-phe-zhee
clothed = nzu-nzu-shki-aum
come = aum-hmu-hmu
come forth = hmu-hmu-aum-shki
comforter = nzu-bnhu-nzu-shki

conclude = shki-shki-aum-zhee-shki
confirming angels = lewhu-nzu-nzu-tuu
confound = phe-lewhu-nzu-aum-phe
contents = tuu-nzu-phe-aum
continual = aum-zhee-aum-ahee
continuance = aum-aum-aum-zhee-aum
corner, corners = nzu-phe-phe-lewhu-aum-hmu
corners = shki-tuu-nzu-tuu
count = bnhu-tuu-tuu-ahee-hmu
covenant = zhee-shki-aum-tuu
cover, covered = nzu-shki-nzu-nzu-hmu
creation = zhee-nzu-aum-aum-zhee
creator = zhee-aum-aum-zhee
crown(s) (object) = aum-zhee-shki-aum
crown (to crown) = aum-zhee-shki-aum
cup, cups = nzu-nzu-shki-shki

D

darkness = shki-zhee-nzu-hmu-aum
daughter = zhee-aum-lewhu-hmu-nzu-aum
day = bnhu-zhee-bnhu-nzu-nzu
death = shki-zhee-shki-zhee
desire = hmu-ayaqox-aum
destroy = shki-bnhu-nzu
destruction = shki-shki-nzu
devour = nzu-aum-zhee-hmu-
diamond = nzu-hmu-hmu-zhee-aum
die = shki-shki-lewhu-shki
dimension shki-shki-nzu-aum
dirt = tuu-shki-bnhu
divide = phe-nzu-shki-tuu

divining = aum-phe-tuu-aum-tuu
do = phe-zhee-bnhu
dog = phe-phe-hwa
door = lewhu-shki-lwehu
dragon = aum-zhee-phe-aum-aum
dream = phe-aum-aum-bnhu

E

eagle = aum-bnhu-aum
earth = shki-lewhu-zhee
eat = tuu-shki
ego = aum-aum-shki-zhee-tuu
elixir = aum-nzu-aum-hmu
empty = shki-aum-phe-nzu-nzu
enchanting = tuu-tuu-hmu-aum
energy = aum-aum-zhee-tuu
enter = bnhu-tuu-bnhu-tuu
entire = hmu-shki-shki
entity = hmu-zhee-zhee-aum-phe
evoking = hmu-shki-shki-nzu
excite = phe-phe-nzu-hmu-tuu
excrement = phe-lewhu-tuu-tuu
experience = shki-aum-phe-aum
explain tuu-zhee-nzu-phe
explode = zhee-tuu-tuu
eye = aum-zhee-tuu-bnhu-zhee

F

face = zhee-tuu-phe-bnhu
faceless = bnhu-zhee-tuu-phe-bnhu
fade = phe-lewhu-bnhu-tuu

fangs = zhee-shki-aum
fat = hmu-tuu
father = aum-zhee-aum-lewhu
fear = shki-aum-nzu-shki
feel = hmu-hmu-aum
fighting = nzu-tuu-tuu-phe
fire = nzu-zhee-nzu
first = zhee-zhee
five = bnhu-zhee
flaming = nzu-zhee-nzu-phe
flow = nzu-hmu-tuu-phe
fly = nzu-nzu-phe-
foolish = phe-tuu-tuu-phe
forget = lewhu-nzu-nzu-phe
foul = shki-bnhu-shki
found = phe-phe-hmu-tuu
four = zhee-hmu
free = aum-tuu-tuu-phe-bnhu
from = phe-lewhu-lewhu-phe
front = nzu-shki-lewhu-bnhu

G

gathering = nzu-hmu-lewhu-tuu-nzu
genius = aum-tuu-nzu-hmu-phe-phe
ghost, = aum-wuz-aum-zhee
god = aum-zhee-aum-zhe-aum
goddess = aum-aum-zhee-zhee-aum
going = phe-aum-nzu-phe
grant = tuu-shki-tuu-zhee
gravity bnhu-zhee-zhee-tuu-phe-phe
great = zhee-phe-lewhu-hmu-lewhu
green = aum-hmu-hmu-zhee-tuu

H

hair = lewhu-bnhu-bnhu-phe
happiness = shki-phe-nzu-nzu-phe
happy = phe-hmu-hmu-tuu-phe
hard = phe-tuu-tuu-hmu-phe
harlot = shki-aum-tuu-zhee
hate = shki-zhee-tuu-aum
have, Having = bnhu-tuu-nzu-nzu-shki
he = shki-hmu-aum-zhee
head = lewhu-aum-aum-bnhu
head (leader) = zhee-aum-nzu-nzu-aum
healing = hmu-aum-aum-phe-zhee-shki
health = phe-phe-shki
hear = bnhu-lewhu-phe-lewhu
heat = tuu-tuu-nzu-nzu-zhee
heaven = aum-aum-shki-hmu-phe
hell = phe-hmu-shki-aum-aum
hidden = tuu-tuu-nzu-phe-nzu
high = phe-hmu-tuu-lewhu-lewhu-nzu
holy = aum-aum-hmu-lewhu
house = shki-aum-shki-phe-aum
how = lewhu-nzu-nzu
human = shki-hmu-hmu-phe
hungry –hmu-phe-phe-shki-shki
hunt = tuu-shki-shki-tuu-tuu
husk = tuu-tuu-nzu-tuu-phe

I

I = aum-tuu-tuu-phe
Illness = nzu-tuu-phe-phe-bnhu
Illuminating = phe-phe-shki-aum-tuu
Imagination = nzu-phe-phe-hmu-shki

In = shki-hmu-hmu
Incense = hmu-nzu-hmu-tuu
Incidentally = aum-shki-zhee-nzu-tuu
Increase = zhee-tuu-hmu-nzu-aum
Infinite, infinity = aum-hmu-hmu-aum-tuu
Information = tuu-aum-bnhu
Inner = phe-tuu-zhee-phe
Insane = zhee-aum-shki-nzu-tuu-nzu
Intuition = shki-aum-aum-zhee-tuu
Invoking = zhee-aum-tuu-bnhu-zhee
Inward = shki-hmu-hmu-zhee-phe
Iron = phe-phe-phe
It = tuu-aum-tuu-tuu-shki-phe
It is done = aum-zhee-hmu-phe-shki-tuu

J

Jackal = hmu-aum-zhee-phe
Jewel = aum-phe-hmu-zhee
Joy = aum-hmu-hmu
Juice = shki-phe-hmu-phe
Jupiter = aum-zhee-ma-aum

K
Knife = shki-phe-phe-tuu
Knight = hmu-phe-aum-phe-tuu

L

Labyrinth = aum-tuu-tuu-phe
Lady = aum-zhee-zhee
Language = phe-hmu-bnhu-tuu
Last = shki-aum-phe-phe-tuu
Laugh = tuu-hmu-nzu

Leg = shki-nzu-nzu-hmu
Leviathan = zhee-hmu-phe-aum-zhee
Life = aum-nzu-nzu-aum-zhee
Lightning flash = aum-shki-bnhu-aum
Like = zhee-nzu-nzu
Lord = shki-aum-nzu-phe-zhee
Lost = nzu-phe-nzu
Loud = hmu-aum-hmu
Love = aum-zhee-bnhu
Low = shki-nzu-nzu-tuu
Loyalty = aum-zhee-bnhu-tuu
Lust = aum-oot-zhee

M

Magician = zhee-aum-tuu-phe
Magic = aum-zhee-tuu-hmu-aum
Magus = zhee-aum-bnhu
Make = aum-shki-shki-aum-tuu
Mars = aum-bnhu-zhee
Matter = zhee-tuu-tuu
Means = hmu-tuu-zhee
Medicine = bnhu-aum-nzu-nzu
Mercury = aum-tuu-tuu-shki-aum
Mind = hmu-aum-shki-hmu
Moon = aum-lstu-zhee
Mother = aum-zhee-aum-tuu
Mouth = tuu-tuu-hmu
Moving = aum-hmu-tuu-nzu
Music = hmu-bnhu-hmu-tuu
Mystical = shki-nzu-nzu

P

Pain = bnhu-shki-tuu
Pentacle = tuu-tuu-aum
Perception = aum-nzu-phe-phe
Permitted = aum-hmu
Phoenix = hmu-phe-zhee-phe-phe
Planet = shki-aum-tuu-bnhu
Plant = aum-tuu-tuu-phe
Pleasure = phe-tuu-tuu-phe
Pierce = nzu-znu-hmu-phe
Poison = lewhu-phe-zhee
Positive = shki-tuu-hmu
Possession = shki-shki-shki-tuu
Potential = shki-nzu
Power = lewhu-aum-zhee
Priest = aum-zhee-phe
Protect, do protection = aum-aum-phe-hmu
Purple = shki-tuu-phe

R

Rain = shki-aum-phe-phe-nzu
Red = aum-nzu-phe-hmu
Religion = lewhu-nzu-nzu-bnhu
Remnant = hmu-phe-tuu
Return = zhee-shki-tuu-tuu
Revealed = tuu-tuu-phe
Ring = aum-zhee—phe-tuu
Rise = tuu-phe-phe-hmu
Ritual = aum-tuu-nzu

S

Sigil = zhee-aum-nzu
Sign = shki-bnhu
Silent = zhee-tuu-phe-phe-tuu

Skin = aum-tuu-tuu-bnhu
Slave = tuu-tuu-phe
Small = tuu-phe-phe-hmu
Smoke = hmu-shki-zhee
Son = aum-tuu-phe
Sorcery = lewhu-bnhu-aum
Shadow = bnhu-hmu-zhee
Sphere = shki-zhee-zhee
Spider = aum-bnhu-nzu-nzu
Square = aum-tuu-nzu
Stand = nzu-phe-phe
Star =zhee-shki-tuu-phe
Sting = tuu-tuu-phe
Stop = phe-nzu-nzu
Storm =zhee-aum-phe-nzu-aum
Strength = phe-aum-nzu
Success = tuu-aum-nzu
Sun = nzu-phe-phe-hmu
Sword = zhee-hmu-aum-shki

T

Thinking = hmu-bnhu-tuu-phe
Three = bnhu-zhee-shki-tuu
Thunder = zhee-tuu-aum-shki
Time = tuu-shki-tuu-aum
Today = shki-tuu-tuu-zhee
Toward = hmu-zhee-bnhu-tuu
Transform = hmu-tuu-tuu-shki
Transform = shki-phe-tuu-nzu
Transformation = hmu-shki-aum
Tree = shki-phe-phe-nzu
Triangle = nzu-phe-nzu-tuu

U

Underneath = phe-tuu-nzu
Unveiled = tuu-shki-bnhu
Us = aum-phe-shki

V

Venus = zhee-aum-phe-tuu
Voice = aum-tuu-nzu
Vortex = nzu-zhee

W

Wait = phe-tuu-nzu
War = zhee-bnhu-tuu
Water = aum-nzu-phe-bnhu
We = bnhu-phe-tuu
Weakness = tuu-aum-nzu
Wealth = zhee-bnhu-aum
What = bnhu-hmu
White = tuu
Why = hmu-tuu-tuu
Will= shki-tuu-nzu
Wolf =shki-zhee-tuu
Womb = phe-lewhu-phe
Word = aum-hmu
World = shki-tuu-zhee

Y

Year = zhee-aum-bnhu
Yes = tuu-shki-tuu
You = phe-tuu-zhee

Vasuh Grammar and Pronunciation

The language of the Vasuh (the Tengu) is a very mystical tool that can be used for the spiritual evolution of the practitioner. Here are a few example of how the language is written versus its pronunciation:

The term *star* as translated from the Vasuh Glossary is *zhee-shki-tuu-phe,* but the pronunciation is in reverse and as follows:

"ehzz-eek-hss-oot-eh-ph"

Thus we find that the **letters** are activated by a reverse pronunciation of the written term. While the reader may find it difficult to remember the terms in the Vasuh Glossary, and then have the task of pronouncing each term in reverse, there is a very simple method of employing the language of dreams that every Initiate must remember,-is that the Vasuh language is based on the principles of mathematics.

Many scholars have stated that the terms found in the Vasuh Glossary are terms that were derived from the practice of telepathy, wherein the shaman would repeat a certain phrase while visualizing and individual and were able to alter reality. The process of how these mantras were created had a lot to do with knowing the mathematical sum of a word regardless of the language spoken. For example, the English term god can be said to have the following mathematical sum: g (7) + o (15) + d (4) = 26. This equation would translate to Nzu (7), plus 1 and 5 equals 6, since "o" is the 15th letter of the English alphabet, it is reduced to its lowest sum, which would be Phe (6), plus Hmu (4). Thus the Vasuh term for god would be *nzu-phe-hmu*. It's pronunciation would then be:

"ooh-zz-nn-eh-ph-you-mmh-ha"

An understanding of this term comes through determining the meaning of each letter.

Nzu = *"Can be used as a protective shield, or to heal cuts and wounds. "*

Phe = *"It affects the quality of the emotions and useful for the arts of levitation."*

Hmu = *"Increases sexual energy and the eyesight"*

Therefore, the English term god is translated into the Vasuh language as *Nzu-Phe-Hmu* meaning, a protective shield affecting the emotions, increasing sexual energy. However, we can get a more exact meaning by reducing the sum of these letters to its lowest value, which would be Nzu (7) + Phe (6) + Hmu (4) equals 17. We would then take 17 and reduce it as follows: Zhee (1) + Nzu (7) equal 8. Therefore, a clear definition of god is equal to 8, or the letter Lewhu, pronounced *ooh-wel*. The attribute of Lewhu are as follows:

"It is used in initiating one to the divine energies of the stars."

Thus, we find that the definition of "god" is the Initiate who uses the divine energies of the stars. It is important that the Initiate of The Cult of Nyarzir understands the importance of using this formulae to translate mystical incantations.

It was by the use of the *mathematical language of dreams,* that an initiate can interpret and communicate with the same forces that he/she are being influenced by, and what deity that they may call upon for clarity, but also transmute their own dna and evolve in being. This is the meaning of the Tablets of Destinies, also known as the Yi Jing.

Editor's Notes

Johuta: Goddess of the Sun and all things pertaining to this realm. She wears a long gown made of gold and has purple skin.

Aixu: Goddess of Mercury and all things pertaining to this realm. She is tall and her face is painted in night and day.

Istu: God of the Moon and all things that correspond to such. He is extremely tall and wears a necklace that glows. Istu is often seen with a scepter that has eight heads on it.

Viyah: Goddess of Venus and all things pertaining to such. Her glory is often arrayed in her long hair, which is filled with a thousand flowers. She has copper skin and usually greets the with a green robe.

Buhqz: Goddess of Mars and all things pertaining to such. Her hair is likened to long strands of fire and her skin is made of iron.

Koqw: God of Jupiter and all things pertaining to such. He often appears as a giant with jet black hair, wearing brass armor.

Quf: God of Saturn and all things pertaining to such. He appears as a man with pale skin, white hair and black lips

Aries: Shara	Libra: Muku
Taurus: Shamhat	Scorpio: Xuz

Gemini: Dakha   Sagittarius: Yuvho

Cancer: Sheba   Capricorn: Muh

Leo: Mezek   Aquarius: Suzha

Virgo: Shupu   Pisces: Nudzuchi

Nine Books of Dreams (Vasuh Letters):

Energies of the Great Bear Constellation

Shamuzi:

Energies of Sirius Constellation

Ninzuwu:

Guardians of Universe B.

The Crow:

Soul of the Adept, the Inner Sun

Zhee corresponds to the crown chakra, which is positioned slightly above the head.

Aum corresponds to the Brow chakra that sits in the center of the forehead.

Tuu corresponds to the throat chakra.

Hmu corresponds to the heart chakra.

Bnhu corresponds to the chakra ruling over the area slightly above the navel.

Phe This mantra relates to the chakra center near you slightly below your navel

Nzu This mantra relates to the base of the spine.

Lewhu corresponds with the chakra that governs over the sexual organs.

Shki corresponds with the Anus chakra. This is the first mantra of the anus

ABOUT THE AUTHOR

Messiah-el Bey is a Ninzuwu Priest. He has been a
practitioner of the Asian and Sumerian mystical arts for
over 12 years.

40235011R00043

Made in the USA
Lexington, KY
28 March 2015